Laura Wilson

First published in Great Britain in 1995
by Hamlyn Children's Books
an imprint of Reed Children's Books,
Michelin House, 81 Fulham Road, London SW3 6RB
and Auckland, Melbourne, Singapore and Toronto.
This paperback edition published in 1996 by
Heinemann Publishers (Oxford) Ltd,
Halley Court, Jordan Hill, Oxford OX2 8EJ

MADRID ATHENS PARIS
FLORENCE PRAGUE WARSAW
PORTSMOUTH NH CHICAGO SAO PAULO
SINGAPORE TOKYO MELBOURNE AUCKLAND
IBADAN GABORONE JOAHANNESBURG

ISBN 0 600 588823

This title is also available in a hardback library edition
(ISBN 0 600 586383)

British Library Cataloguing-in-Publication Data
A catalogue record for this book is available from the
British Library

Printed in Hong Kong

Conceived and produced by Breslich & Foss, London
Art Director: Nigel Osborne
Design: Paul Cooper
Illustrations: John James
Photography: Garth Blore, Nigel Bradley and Miki Slingsby

Replica furniture at the Weald and Downland
Open Air Museum made by Roger Champion

CONTENTS

THE TUDOR MONARCHS

The Tudor period lasted from 1485 to 1603. England was at peace after years of civil wars, and under the Tudors it became richer and more powerful than ever before. English sailors explored newly discovered countries and set up trade routes, the English Church broke away from the Catholic Church in Rome (*see below*) and several of the greatest works of literature were written.

The Tudor monarchs were some of the most splendid in England's history. They had much more power than modern kings and queens, because they decided how the country was run, whether it should go to war, and what religion their subjects should follow. During the early part of the Tudor period, England was a Catholic country. However, there were some people who did not like the Catholic Church. These people were called Protestants, because they protested against the Catholic Church and wanted the organization of the church and its services to be changed.

Henry VIII

Henry VII, who was crowned in 1485, was the first Tudor king. Henry VIII (*see left*) became king of England in 1509 aged 18, on the death of his father. He wanted to have a son as his heir to the throne, but although his wife Catherine of Aragon had many children, only one, Mary, survived.

Henry fell in love with Anne Boleyn and wanted a divorce from Catherine so that he could marry her and have a son. No one could get divorced unless the Pope, who was head of the Catholic Church, gave permission, and this he refused to do. Henry decided that he would take charge of the church in England, so that he could grant himself a divorce. He married Anne Boleyn in 1533 and in 1534 an Act was passed declaring Henry to be head of the English Church. Although he refused to obey the Pope, Henry did not become a Protestant. However, there were many English Protestants at this time, and Henry's youngest children, Elizabeth and Edward, were brought up in that religion.

Henry was disappointed when Anne gave birth to the Princess Elizabeth instead of the son he wanted. He claimed that Anne had been unfaithful to him, and had her beheaded in 1536. He then married Jane Seymour. She gave birth to a son, Edward, in 1537, but died soon afterwards. There were no surviving children from Henry's other three marriages.

Edward VI

Edward VI (*see above*) became king on his father's death in 1547. He was only nine, so his uncle, Edward Seymour, became the Lord Protector to help him rule. Edward VI was a Protestant, and he wanted England to be a Protestant country.

Mary I

Mary I (*see right*) became queen in 1553. Like her mother, Catherine of Aragon, she was Catholic, and wanted to turn England back into a Catholic country. Mary persecuted many Protestants, including Elizabeth, who she locked up in the Tower of London. Mary wanted an heir, but although she married Philip II of Spain, they had no children.

Elizabeth I

When Elizabeth I (*see right*) became queen in 1558, England became a Protestant country again. Some Catholics thought that Henry VIII's marriage to Anne Boleyn had been illegal, and they did not accept Elizabeth as queen. They said that Mary, Queen of Scots, the Catholic granddaughter of Henry VIII's sister Margaret and James IV of Scotland, should be queen and plotted to kill Elizabeth and put Mary on the throne. The plot was discovered and Mary and her supporters were executed.

Elizabeth never married, although several times she made plans to do so. When she died, without an heir, in 1603, James VI of Scotland, the son of Mary, Queen of Scots, became King James I of England.

Exploration

The first English expedition to the "New World" (America) was in 1497. Later, Elizabeth I encouraged sailors to go on voyages to trade goods. Sailors were given "letters of marque" which allowed them to attack and rob the ships of hostile nations, like pirates.

The Spanish had conquered much of South and Central America by the mid-16th century and English sailors often attacked Spanish ships returning from America with treasure.

The Armada

Elizabeth's Protestant religion and her beheading of Mary, Queen of Scots angered Mary I's husband Philip II of Spain. Although Elizabeth tried to avoid war with Spain, her seamen still attacked Spanish ships. Philip II ordered a large fleet of ships called the Armada to be built, and they set sail in 1588 to invade England. They had to anchor off the French coast because bad weather stopped them crossing the Channel. Ships in Elizabethan times were wooden and the English surprised the Spanish during the night by sending burning ships amongst their fleet. Afraid that their own ships would catch fire, the Spaniards scattered. The next day the Spaniards were defeated in a sea battle. They were forced to sail around Great Britain and Ireland to return to Spain, and many of their remaining ships were wrecked. The defeat of the Armada made Elizabeth more popular than ever before.

Left: *The battle of the Armada.*

LIFE IN TUDOR ENGLAND

Under the Tudors, England was an important trading centre and its merchants made a lot of money selling English goods, especially wool and cloth, to other countries. Although the increased business meant that more people came to live in the towns, most people still lived in the country.

Roads

Most people spent their lives in the same parish and never travelled beyond it. A system of roads linked up the villages and towns, and they were mainly used by people travelling to and from market or

driving cows, pigs and sheep to the butcher. Most people travelled on foot, although some rode horses. Coaches were very rare in Tudor times, but if rich people were old or ill they could travel in a litter. This was a covered seat held up on two horizontal shafts extending in front and behind it. Servants would pick up the shafts and carry the person along in the chair between them.

Tudor roads were made of earth and gravel. They were bumpy, and, when it rained, very muddy. A law was passed that every cottager and householder had to spend six days every year repairing the roads. Men who owned land did not have to do this work themselves, but had to send two men to do it instead.

Even when the weather was dry and the roads were good, travelling was slow. People on foot might manage 10 miles in one day if they did not have too many hills to climb. On horseback, 30 miles a day might be covered. However, rich and important people did not travel more quickly than poor ones – it was considered smart to travel slowly, not fast. When Tudor kings and queens went on a "royal progress", accompanied by guards, servants and goods, they rarely covered over 10 miles a day. At night, travelling monarchs stayed at the houses of the nobility. Ordinary travellers could get a meal and a bed at a roadside inn, like the one shown above.

Below: *Country women travelling to market.*

Towns

Many Tudor towns were surrounded by walls on three sides, with a river on the fourth *(see below)*. The walls had gates which were locked at dusk. If anyone wanted to enter or leave the town after that, they had to give a reason to the officer at the gatehouse.

Towns were noisy, crowded and smelly. The houses were made of wood and built very close together on narrow streets. The rooms inside were small and dark. There were many shops, including bakers, shoe-makers and candle-makers. Outside the butchers' shops, cows and pigs wandered about until it was time for them to be killed, because there was no way to keep meat fresh.

The Country Landscape

The countryside was full of big open fields. There were a few stone walls dividing them, but no hedges. Instead, there were patches of trees and shrubs called shaws *(see page 11)*.

Villages

Tudor villages had small cottages for the husbandmen (farm workers) and their families. Farm work, known as husbandry, was the most common job for men in Tudor times. Most villages had a mansion house nearby, which was owned by a nobleman. The village belonged to him, and the villagers not only worked for him but also rented patches of land for growing their crops. Land was also owned by yeoman farmers. Although they owned their own house and farmland and had men working for them, they were not as rich or powerful as lords of the manor.

Villages did not have shops, because everyone grew their own crops and kept farm animals on the "common land" which was shared by the villagers. They had mills for grinding flour to make into bread, and pedlars travelled from village to village selling small items such as ribbons and laces.

Above centre: *This tapestry is one of a series of four, known as The Seasons. It is called Summer and shows husbandmen reaping corn and shearing sheep.*

Left: *Sheep and cows being driven to market.*

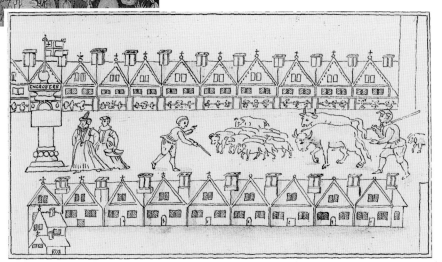

THE FAMILY

The year is 1590, the thirty-second year of Elizabeth I's reign. Harry Bailly is 50 years old. He is lucky to have lived so long – lack of medical knowledge means that only one person in ten lives past the age of 40. He is content because he owns a good farm and has three sons, so his name will be carried on and the house and land will remain in his family. Harry's first wife, Agnes, died in childbirth and he is now married to Alice.

Above: *An Elizabethan family.*

When people got married, it was for life – they could not get divorced. The Tudors believed that a man ruled over his family in the same way as their monarch ruled over the kingdom; it was the law of God, as well as the law of the land that he should do so. Women had very few rights, and children, no rights at all. For example, there was no law to stop a man from beating his wife and children – in fact, it was thought to be his duty to punish them, in the same way that God sometimes punished people for doing wrong.

HARRY BAILLY

Harry is a yeoman – a farmer who owns his own land, but is not of "gentle" or noble birth. He is an important person in his local community, who can be summoned to do jury service (*see page 35*). Yeomen like Harry also do unpaid work as churchwardens (*see page 36*).

Harry farms 75 acres of land, growing crops and keeping cows, sheep and pigs. His eldest son Thomas helps him, and he has two labourers, John and Richard (*see opposite*).

ALICE BAILLY

Alice was 25 years old when she married Harry. She is now 36 years old and has had three boys. The eldest, William, and the youngest, Robert, survive. Her second son, also called Robert, died at the age of three months (it is common to give a baby the same name as an older child who has died). While Harry does the heavier work of the farm, Alice is responsible for the house, garden and farmyard.

THOMAS AND KATHERINE BAILLY

Thomas is the son of Harry's first wife Agnes. He is 22 and married Katherine last year. They have a son, Edward, who is six months old. As Thomas is the eldest son, the house and land will be his when Harry dies. Until then, he and Katherine live with Harry and Alice, and Thomas helps Harry on the farm. Katherine, who is 20, looks after Edward and helps in the house. The system of leaving everything to the eldest son is called primogeniture.

WILLIAM AND ROBERT BAILLY

William, aged 10, and Robert, aged seven, are Alice's sons. Their prospects are not as good as those of their half-brother Thomas, since they will have to find some other means of making their living. Thomas, as the eldest son, will be expected to help them as much as he can.

Left: *Pottery jugs and wooden platters. Wooden household articles like this were called "treen".*

JOHN TURNER AND RICHARD HILL

John, aged 20, and Richard, aged 25, are husbandmen who work on the farm. Their working hours are fixed by law. In summer, they must work from five am until seven or eight pm, with a total of two and a half hours' break, and in winter they must work from dawn until dusk, with one and a half hours' break. Their maximum wage is also fixed: if Harry was caught paying them extra, they would all be imprisoned and fined. Richard would like to marry a local girl, Maud, but they must wait until he has more money and a place to live – at the moment, he and John live in the Baillys' house.

THE HOUSE

The Baillys' house, which is smaller than a mansion, is called a manor house. Many yeoman farmers live in houses like this. They are fortunate because many Elizabethans cannot afford such a house and live in one- or two-roomed cottages with earth floors. Houses are made of wood, brick, flint or stone – whatever is available locally, as these materials are too heavy to be transported very far. The Baillys' house has a framework of oak. Oak wood is often chosen for building because it is strong, and there are many oak

trees in England. Once the framework has been put up, the spaces between the timbers need to be filled. On the bottom storey of the Baillys' house brick has been used for this, and wattle and daub for the top storey. The wattle is made of stems of woven hazel, and the daub, which is plastered over it to make a smooth surface, is made of clay, lime, cow-dung, chopped straw and water.

Like most houses built after 1550, the Baillys' house has a chimney. The house where Alice grew up was built in 1490 and had no chimney. The hearth was in the middle of the floor and smoke escaped through gaps in the roof. When Alice married Harry, she was pleased that her new home had a brick chimney.

Above: *Firewood is stored in the lean-to.*

Above: *The house, garden and farmyard.*

Right: *Front view of the house. None of the windows have glass. Shutters (see page 13) are put up at night to keep out rain. The shutters cannot be put up in the daytime because they would block out all the light, so if it rains during the day, the water comes inside the house. Window glass is expensive, but it is becoming popular, and Harry wants to install some in his house.*

Left: *The Baillys' garden (see page 18).*

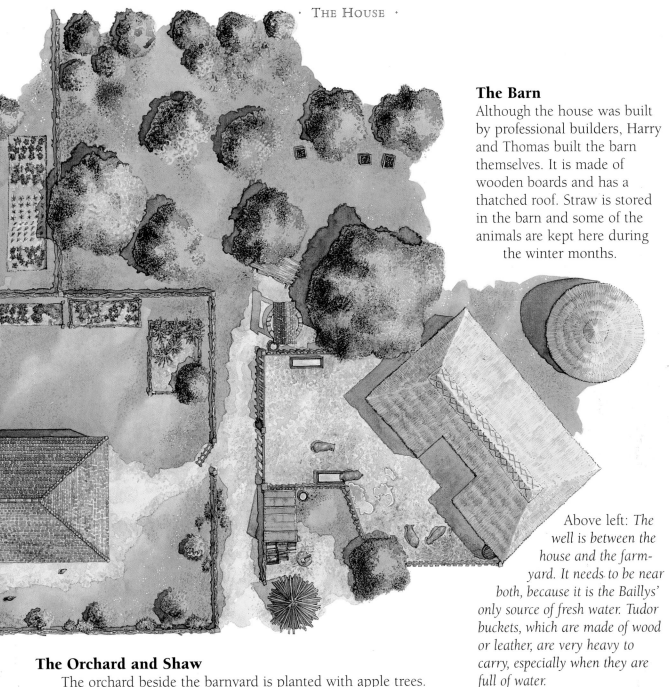

The Barn

Although the house was built by professional builders, Harry and Thomas built the barn themselves. It is made of wooden boards and has a thatched roof. Straw is stored in the barn and some of the animals are kept here during the winter months.

Above left: The well is between the house and the farm-yard. It needs to be near both, because it is the Baillys' only source of fresh water. Tudor buckets, which are made of wood or leather, are very heavy to carry, especially when they are full of water.

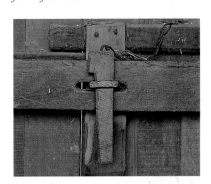

Above: The barn door is bolted shut with a wooden peg.

The Orchard and Shaw

The orchard beside the barnyard is planted with apple trees. The shaw (*see page 7*) at the top of the orchard separates it from the road. It is planted with oak and ash trees, grown for their wood, as well as crab apple trees, holly, hawthorn, wild cherry and wild roses. The grass is full of wild flowers which Katherine sometimes picks to decorate the house. Red squirrels and birds live in the shaw, and it provides fire-wood for the house.

Inside the House

This is a plan of the inside of the Baillys' house. On the ground floor (*shown on page 13*) there are four rooms: the room on the left-hand side with the brick floor and table is the kitchen, the middle room is the parlour and the two rooms on the right are storerooms. The bedrooms are upstairs. Elizabethan homes do not have much furniture, and the Baillys have only a couple of tables, a cupboard, some stools and their beds and chests. Stools and small tables are often made with three legs, not four, because it makes them easier to stand on the bumpy floor.

Above: *The upstairs rooms do not have ceilings, but are open to the rafters.*

Below: *The first floor.*

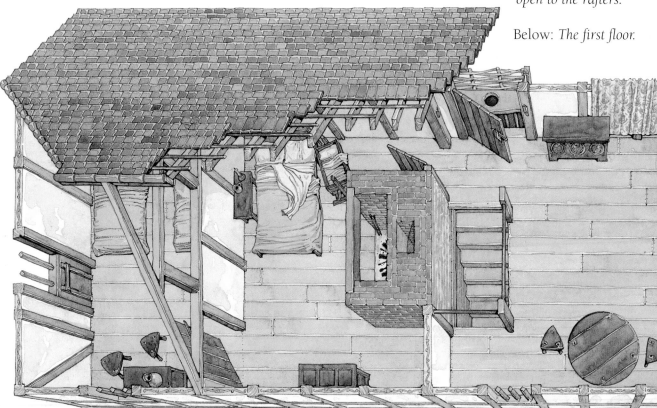

Bedrooms

Harry and Alice and their children sleep in the large room on the right-hand side of the first floor. Elizabethan houses do not have corridors and landings. This means that people are always having to walk through other people's bedrooms, so no one gets much privacy.

Thomas, Katherine and baby Edward sleep in the middle room, and John and Richard sleep in the room on the left-hand side of the first floor.

Above: *The Baillys' garderobe (toilet) is opposite the top of the stairs (see page 43).*

Right: *The ground floor.*

Left: *The wooden stairs are quite steep, more like a ladder with steps and a handrail than a staircase.*

 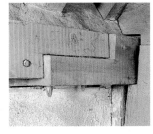

Above: *The inside of the roof. The outside is covered in clay tiles. Each tile is hung over the roof frame with pegs.*

Above: *Jointed wall beams. The joints are held in place by wooden pegs like the ones shown here.*

Below: *The kitchen floor in the Baillys' house is made of brick, but the other floors in the downstairs rooms are made of beaten clay which is strewn with rushes. The floors of the upstairs rooms are made of wooden boards.*

Building the House

The main timbers of the house are oak *(see page 10)* and they are held together by different sorts of joints. When a house like this one is going to be built, the builders first cut down trees and chop off the branches. Then they saw up the trunks into long pieces of wood which can be shaped into beams. The builders cut joints in the

beams so that they can be easily fitted together with other beams, like a large jigsaw-puzzle. When all the joints are finished, the builders lay the beams flat out on the floor and put them together like a kit. They assemble each wall and part of the roof separately before hoisting them upright and fixing them all together.

Above: *Window shutters. These shutters slide up and down in grooves on either side of the window. When the shutters are closed they are held in place by a rope at the top and a peg at the bottom.*

EARLY MORNING

The Baillys' alarm clock is their cockerel, which crows at dawn every morning. They do not have electric light, so they need to get up at dawn to make the most of the daylight. Harry and Thomas say their prayers and take down the shutters to let light into the house (see page 13). After she has dressed (see page 16) and said the Lord's Prayer, Alice goes downstairs to light the fire. Richard and John have fetched logs for her. The Baillys need to have plenty of logs and kindling wood all year round (see right) for cooking food and heating their house. In spite of the chimney, the inside walls of the house are darkened by smoke from the fire.

Alice uses a tinderbox to light the fire. The word "tinder" means any material which catches fire and burns easily, such as straw or paper, and a tinderbox is a box containing some straw, a piece of steel and a flint. To get a light, Alice must strike the flint with the steel until it makes a spark which will set the straw on fire.

William and Robert come downstairs and have a quick breakfast before leaving for their two-mile walk to school (see page 28). They must leave at five o'clock in the summer and six o'clock in the winter in order to get to school on time. The Baillys do not eat much for breakfast, which is usually only a piece of bread and a cup of ale each.

Above: *The fireplace. Alice's cooking pot is attached to a "pot crane" so that she can move it on top of the fire or away from it to control the temperature of her cooking. The fireplace, which is made of brick, has a bake-oven built into the chimney stack for baking bread.*

"**Where is my satchel, my penknife and my book? I must come to school by times [early], I shall be whipped else.**" William

Left: *Firewood is stacked like this so that it doesn't get too wet. John and Richard use axes to chop these pieces of wood into small logs which can be put on the fire.*

The Farmyard

After breakfast, the men go out to start work on the farm. Katherine looks after Edward and Alice goes into the farmyard to feed the hens and geese *(see page 21)* and collect their eggs. She also has to feed the young pigs *(see below)*. Older pigs are usually let loose in the woods where they can find food for themselves. Alice and Katherine milk the cows and take the milk indoors to be made into butter and cheese.

Above: *The Baillys' barnyard. It is surrounded by a wooden fence which prevents the animals from straying.*

Left: *John fetches water from the well for Alice. He lowers the bucket into the water on the pulley, and pulls on the rope to lift it back up again.*

Above: *Richard fetches the logs in this wooden wheelbarrow which he made himself.*

Left: *The Baillys' pigs are smaller and thinner than modern pigs, with longer snouts and dark, bristly coats.*

GETTING DRESSED

I t does not take long for the Baillys to get dressed in the morning. The men sleep in their shirts and the women in their chemises (similar to a blouse) and, as they do not have any underwear, all they need do to be ready for the day is pull on their other clothes over the top.

Every Elizabethan, from the richest to the poorest, wears the

same basic clothes. Men wear a shirt and doublet (a close-fitting garment like a jacket), and hose, which are like very thick tights. The hose are sometimes padded, like the ones shown in the picture on the left. The padding might be horsehair, cotton or wool rags. Some people even pad their hose with bran, but this is not a good idea because it spills out if the hose get torn. All women wear long-sleeved dresses with skirts that come down to the ground. No noblewoman would ever show her arms or ankles, but women who need to do cooking and gardening, like Alice and Katherine, sometimes roll up their sleeves and hitch up their skirts a little while they work.

Most men and women wear a small ruff around their neck and something on their head – men usually wear a hat or cap and women wear a hood or hat. If they meet a woman, or if anybody mentions the queen's name, polite men like Harry and Thomas take off their hats as a sign of respect.

Men who do not have to do physical work, like priests, merchants and the teachers at William and Robert's school, wear long coats called gowns which are trimmed with fur. Harry has one of these gowns, which he puts on when he goes to church or into town. When people see the gown, they know that Harry is a person of some importance.

Below: *These shoes are made of leather. Other materials used for making shoes are velvet, silk and cloth. Shoe soles are made from leather or cork.*

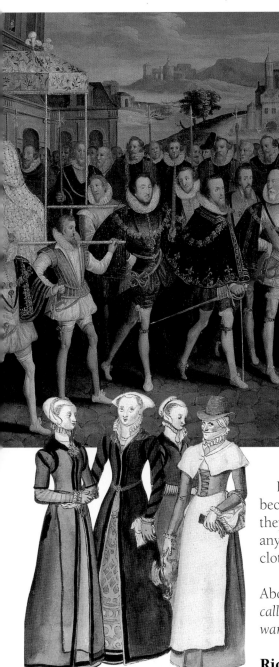

Sumptuary Laws

Elizabethans are not allowed to wear what they like. There are a number of laws, called Sumptuary Laws, which make sure that people dress according to their position in society. Lower-class people may wear clothes made of cotton or wool, but they are not allowed to wear rich materials such as velvet or silk, or any material that is red or purple in colour. If they do, they will be fined. Husbandmen like Richard and John are not allowed to wear any hose worth more than ten pence a yard, or they will be put in the stocks *(see page 46)* for three days. Another law says that all men over the age of six, apart from the nobility, must wear a woollen cap on Sundays and holy days *(see page 40)*. Men who do not wear a cap on these days have to pay a fine. This law was passed to give cappers (cap-makers) plenty of work and protect their jobs.

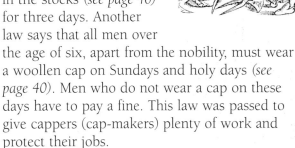

People do not think there is anything strange about these laws, because they believe that a person's clothes should indicate what they are, just as army uniforms show us the rank of the soldier. In any case, even if poor people were allowed to wear silk and velvet clothes, they could not afford to buy them.

Above right: *John and Richard wear clothes like these. Woollen jackets called jerkins keep them warm in winter. When the weather grows warmer, they take off their jerkins and doublets and work in their shirts.*

Rich People's Clothes

Wealthy people wear elaborate clothes which are heavy and stiff and make it difficult to move easily. The clothes show that they do not have to work for their living. In the 1590s, both men and women wear large ruffs around their necks. Starch, which is known as "the devil's liquor", is used to make the ruffs stiff. All fashionable ladies wear a French farthingale, which is a wheel-shaped cage that goes under their skirts and makes them stick out in a circle around the waist. Queen Elizabeth and her ladies are wearing them in the centre picture. Those who cannot afford a proper farthingale wear a "bumroll" to give their skirts the right shape. A bumroll is a padded tube which is tied around the waist.

Top: *Queen Elizabeth and her court.*

Above: *For work, Alice wears clothes like the ones shown on the right. The wide-brimmed hat keeps the sun off her face when she is working outside. On special occasions, she wears a dress and hood like the ones on the left.*

THE GARDEN

Alice goes into the garden to choose some vegetables and herbs for lunch. Like most housewives, Alice uses the garden to grow fruit and vegetables for her family. She also grows herbs which she uses both as food and as medicine (*see page 37*). Although Alice grows flowers

such as violets and primroses, they are there not to be looked at, but to be eaten. Instead of a lawn, Alice's garden has a number of plots of earth for plants to grow in, with grassy paths between them so that she can tend to them easily. Vegetables or "worts" are an important part of most people's diets (*see page 30*), and Alice picks a small cabbage, a leek, an onion and some garlic to make a "pottage" or stew, and some salad leaves, fennel, herbs and flowers for a "sallet" (a word meaning not only salad, but any vegetable dish, whether raw or cooked). She also picks some flowers and herbs for strewing over the rushes on the floor of the house to make it smell nice.

Above: *Watering can.*

Below: *Alice puts sticks across her young plants to stop rabbits eating them.*

Fruit and Vegetables

Alice has pear trees in her garden and apple trees in the orchard. She also has damson trees and plum trees, and grows strawberries and gooseberries. She has heard of the new "apricocks" (apricots) which have come recently from Portugal, and the "apples of love"

"The sun did not shine here this day, for the grass is yet with dew. The garden is marvellous cool and the birds chatter their sweet tunes." Alice

Right: *Alice makes tea from a herb called hyssop. This plot of earth is surrounded by a small wattle (woven) fence.*

(tomatoes) from Mexico, and is very curious to see and taste them. She has never seen an orange, as these are imported from Portugal and so expensive that only rich, fashionable people eat them. She once tasted a potato, but she did not think much of it and would certainly not consider growing them in her garden.

Alice agrees with the physicians (doctors) that eating raw fruit makes people ill, and scolds her sons if they try to eat any raw fruit, even strawberries. She makes sure that it is either baked in a pie or boiled and made into a pottage.

Gardening

Alice sows most of her seeds in March and April, rotating the different crops from plot to plot to keep the soil fertile. Sometimes she does not sow any seeds in a plot, but leaves it to "lie fallow" for a year in order to rest it. Both animal and human manure (*see page 43*) are spread on the garden to fertilize the soil.

Besides leeks, garlic, peas and parsnips, Alice also grows skirrets (similar to parsnips), collards and kale (types of cabbage). As well as herbs such as sage, thyme, rosemary, parsley, chives and lavender, she grows Good King Henry, which is like spinach, summer savoury, which has a peppery taste, and Alexander, which tastes like celery. She grows comfrey and wormwood to use as medicines, and woad and weld to use as dyes for her wool (*see page 23*). Some of the vegetables and herbs that Alice grows in her garden are shown below.

Above: *Onions are very popular. Alice boils them with salt, sugar and raisins. With a poached egg on top, they make a good meal.*

Above: *Alice collects borage to put into her herb and flower salads, along with primroses, violets and gillyflowers.*

Above: *Alice has grown these leeks for their seeds, which she stores and sows in the spring.*

Above: *If the Baillys feel hungry, they chew dill leaves and seeds to stop their stomachs rumbling.*

19

HOUSEWIFERY

After she has fed the animals, Alice returns to the house. She and Katherine have a great deal of work to do indoors. Tudor women have particular kinds of jobs, which are known as "housewifery". These include milking the cows and

making butter and cheese, looking after the hens and geese, the bees and the garden and selling produce at the market, as well as preserving and cooking food, and making clothes, soap and candles. Many women also help their husbands during busy times on the farm, such as harvest time.

"There is no time to chat and prattle, I must look to the kine [cows] and set all fair about the house." Alice

This morning, Alice has noticed that the rushes strewn on the floor are old and dirty, so she sweeps them out and goes to get some fresh ones. However, Tudor women do not clean their houses very often, and they only wash the family's clothes and bedsheets three or four times a year. When Alice and Katherine do the washing, they take the dirty things to a nearby river and soap them with homemade soap (see page 42) and then trample on them with bare feet and beat them against stones to get them clean. It is exhausting work and takes a long time. Afterwards, they bring the wet clothes back to the house and drape them over bushes or spread them out flat on the grass to dry.

Above: *Milking is done by hand. Cows give more milk during the summer months, when there is plenty of grass for them to eat.*

Left: *Churning milk to make butter is hard work. If her butter looks pale, Alice uses bright yellow marigold petals to dye it so that it will sell better at the market.*

Right: *Alice's storeroom.*

Candles

Candles and rushlights are the only means the Baillys have of lighting their home. Candles are made from beeswax *(see right)*. The wick, which is a piece of coarse thread, is dipped into wax and removed and hung up until the wax has set. This process is continued until the candle is fat enough to be able to burn for a long time. Candles last longer and give out a brighter light than rushlights, which are made from rushes dipped into melted animal fat.

Left: *Candle-making equipment. The two black jugs are full of wax, and the candles are dipped into them and then hung on twigs across this wooden frame so that the wax can set. There are finished candles in the grey pot and a lighted candle is fixed to an iron wall-holder.*

Below: *The hens and cockerel are allowed to wander about where they like during the day. At night, they climb a tiny ladder up the side of the barn into the hen loft, where they sleep.*

Bees

The beehives are in a quiet part of the garden where they will not be disturbed. Alice keeps bees both for their honey and their wax, which she uses for candles. Hives are either made out of woven straw or out of woven wicker daubed with clay *(see above)*. Alice's bees are black bees, not striped ones. She collects their honey every autumn.

Above: *Alice keeps the geese in the orchard. If there is a feast (see page 40) she might kill and roast one as a treat. The grease from the dead goose helps to keep the farming equipment running smoothly. Geese are good watchdogs because they honk and hiss when they see someone coming.*

SPINNING AND WEAVING

A s soon as she has had breakfast and fed the baby, Katherine starts her spinning. All Tudor women, whether they are rich or poor, spend a lot of time spinning wool and making clothes. In the summer, when the sheep have been sheared, some of the wool is sold and the rest is collected in baskets and brought into the house for Alice or Katherine to spin. Wool that has come straight from a sheep is dirty and matted, and it has to be washed and combed out before being spun into thread. Alice and Katherine also spin flax from flax plants to make linen thread. They take this to a weaver, who weaves it into cloth on a loom. Alice and Katherine then make the cloth into clothes for the family (see page 16).

"I thank God that I have cloth to make two new shirts, and the ruffs and bands [collars] are made ready." Katherine

Right: *This prickly teasel head is used for teasing the wool to get rid of lumps and get all the strands running in the same direction so it can be made into thread.*

Right: *Alice is using this spindle to spin her wool. She takes single strands from the mass of wool which is held on a stick called a distaff, and twists them together to form one long strand, which she winds onto the spindle.*

22

Far left: *Katherine uses the spinning wheel, which is known as the "great wheel". A spinning wheel is really a spindle which is turned round by the large, hand-driven wheel. Katherine turns the wheel with her right hand and holds the yarn in her left hand. As she turns the wheel the fibres twist together to make thread, which winds round the spindle.*

Above: *A pot of teasel heads and a basket full of different coloured wool. Katherine uses plants and flowers from the garden to dye the wool.*

Dyeing Wool

These differently coloured wools (*see right*) show some of the colours that are available to Alice and Katherine. The pink wool at the top is made from imported brazil wood dye and fermented urine. The brazil wood dye is made from American trees with red wood and the urine is used as a bleach to turn the red into a cerise pink. Weld from the Baillys' garden is used to make the mustard-yellow colour of the wool next to it. Weld is a plant with greenish-yellow flowers which are used to make a yellow-coloured dye. The dark brown wool is made from walnut, and the two light brown wools from the root of the madder plant. The pale orange wool is coloured with onion skins, and the yellow and green ones are made from weld mixed with woad. Woad, like weld, is a common plant in Elizabethan gardens, and its leaves give a blue dye which makes a green colour when mixed with weld. As the yellow and green wools show, the amounts of woad and weld in the mixture can be varied to give very different results.

23

HUSBANDRY

Men's work is known as "husbandry" just as women's work is known as "housewifery". Harry, Thomas and their husbandmen Richard and John work on the farm all year round, growing the crops and looking after the animals. It is hard, physical labour because all the jobs have to be done by hand, with only simple tools for help.

Above: A wooden ox yoke. Harry keeps oxen to pull his plough. One of the men walks behind the plough to steer the oxen.

Right: Harry's horse pulls the cart, and sometimes the harrow. Two-wheeled carts like the one shown are the most common type of vehicle.

Spring

The work the men do depends on the time of year. In the early months of the year, the lambs are born and the ploughing is done. Then the ground is harrowed *(see page 46)* in order to break up any large lumps of soil that are left after ploughing. Next the wheat, oats and barley are planted. The seeds are not actually dug into the ground, but Richard and John walk across the fields, scattering them in handfuls. At this time of year, Robert and William are kept home from school so that they can throw stones at any birds who try to eat the seeds.

"This ten days, thanks be to God, we have had very fair and dry weather for our harvest, which is great [large]."
Thomas

Left: *When the men go out to work in the fields, they fill this leather container with ale and take it with them.*

Summer and Autumn

When the new grass comes through, the cows are let out into the fields. During May and June the sheep are sheared and any land that has been left to lie fallow (*see page 19*) has to be weeded before it is ploughed. After this, the haymaking and harvesting must be done. The crops are harvested with scythes and brought to the barn to be threshed. The purpose of threshing is to make the grain fall out of the husks. This is done by beating it with a flail, which is a long pole with a piece of free-swinging leather attached to it, rather like a whip. Then the grains and husks need to be separated from each other. This is done by winnowing. The mixed grains and husks are put into a winnowing basket and tossed. Husks are lighter than grains, so they blow away and only the grain is left. Thomas takes it to the mill to be ground into flour so that Alice and Katherine can make bread. Richard and John pick the ripe fruit from the trees and collect logs and kindling wood so that there will be enough fuel for the winter months.

Winter

The oxen, horses and cows spend the winter months in the barn. Harry slaughters some cows and pigs in November, and Alice and Katherine preserve the meat. The December weather makes it impossible for the men to work in the fields, but Richard and John go "hedging and ditching" and mend the roads (*see page 6*). Harry looks over all the farming equipment to see what must be repaired before work begins again.

Above: *Corn stooks. At harvest time the crops are cut down and made into sheaves (bundles). Several sheaves are propped together in a stook so that they will be quite dry before they are threshed.*

Above: *A rake, a fork, a scythe and a winnowing basket. The men make all the farm tools themselves.*

Left: *The barn is thatched with straw, which is held in place with lengths of hazel wood. Richard chops wood to repair the thatch and mend the barnyard fence which was damaged when a piglet got loose.*

Right: *The haystack. Pigs and cows are slaughtered in November because there is no food available for them in winter apart from hay.*

BABIES AND CHILDREN

Thomas and Katherine's son Edward is six months old. Edward was baptised as soon as possible after he was born. This was so that if he died, he would be able to go to heaven. Many babies die during, or soon after, birth, and many who survive do not live longer than one year.

Like all babies, Edward is swaddled, or wrapped up in bandages known as "swaddling bands", in order to stop his arms and legs breaking or growing crooked. When Edward was first born, he was swaddled from head to foot so that he could not move his arms or legs, and Katherine, like many Elizabethan mothers, used to hook one of the bandages over a nail in the wall so that he could hang there out of harm's way while she got on with her work. When Edward was four months old, his arms were freed. Edward's swaddling bands are changed only once a day, so he is very smelly. When Katherine changes the bands, she bounces him on her knee and plays with him, hiding a brightly coloured stone behind her back and saying "Handy, dandy, prickly, prandy, which hand will you have?" to make him laugh. When it is his bedtime, she rocks his cradle (*see opposite*) and sings a lullaby to help him sleep.

Above: *This little girl has a silver rattle with a pink coral teething stick attached to it. Coral was used because it was thought to be good for sore gums and because it was a lucky charm which was supposed to prevent illness. Only rich children had toys like this rattle – other children had homemade toys, or, as a special treat, a doll or drum bought from a pedlar.*

Parents and Children

Harry and Alice, like other Elizabethan parents, believe that children are sinful when they are born, and that, in order to make them grow up into good Christians, they must be strict with them. If Harry thinks that Alice is spoiling the children and letting them have their own way, he gets angry. He quotes from the Bible: "He that spareth the rod hateth his son".

William and Robert are very respectful to their parents. They call their mother "Madam" and their father "Sir" and kneel down to ask for their blessing every morning and evening.

Above left: *When the family has a meal, William and Robert eat their food standing up while the adults sit on stools.*

Left: *It is difficult to cuddle a baby in swaddling bands. These two are so tightly wrapped up that they look as stiff as boards.*

Children's Clothes

Boys and girls both wore petticoats and an apron until the age of five, when boys were put into breeches and girls into tight corset-like bodices in order to mould their figures into a fashionable shape *(see left)*. There were no special designs for children's clothes – they were simply smaller versions of what the adults wore.

"I salute my father and mother and say God give you good morrow [good morning] father, and father, give me your blessing if it please you."
Robert

Right: *Edward's cradle is beside his parents' bed. The mattress is a small sack filled with straw. Every morning Katherine takes the wet, dirty straw out and replaces it with fresh straw. The sheets are made of unbleached linen.*

Riddles

Besides outdoor sports and games *(see page 38)*, William and Robert, like many Tudor children, love telling riddles. This is one of their favourites:

What does it mean? *(The answer is on page 48)*.

Two legs sat upon three legs
With one leg in his lap;
In comes four legs
And runs away with one leg;
Up jumps two legs,
Catches up three legs,
Throws it after four legs,
And makes him bring back one leg.

AT SCHOOL

Left: *This is the Edward VI Grammar School in Stratford upon Avon where the playwright William Shakespeare was taught.*

L ike the sons of many yeomen, merchants, skilled craftsmen and squires, William and Robert go to grammar school. Noblemen's sons are educated at home by tutors. Boys from poor families attend the parish school when they can be

spared from work at home. Harry's labourers, John and Richard, can both read and write a little, and they know enough Latin to say the Lord's Prayer. Girls' education is different from boys', because it is considered more important for a girl to know about housewifery than scholarly subjects like Latin. Girls do not attend school, but they are often taught how to read, write and do simple sums. Both Alice and Katherine can read and write, and Alice keeps the household accounts.

Robert has just started to go with his elder brother to the grammar school, which takes pupils from the age of seven as long as they can read, write and say their catechism (a series of questions and answers about God and the church). Before that, he attended a "petty" or infant school.

School starts early in the morning (*see page 14*) and does not finish until 5pm. There is a break between 11am and 1pm for lunch. Boys go to school every day except Sunday, and their only holidays are the holy days (*see page 40*), two weeks at Easter and two at Christmas. At William and Robert's school there are 60 boys in one classroom, with two masters to teach them.

"If you have not learned your lesson by heart you shall be whipped four blows with the rods." William

Spelling

William and Robert do not have to learn spellings, because Tudor English did not have a rule that one spelling of a word was right and all the others were wrong. For example, the word "go" could be spelt go or goe, the word "ink" could be spelt ink, inke, ynk, or ynke, and William and Robert could write their surname as Bailly, Baillie, Baylie or Bayly.

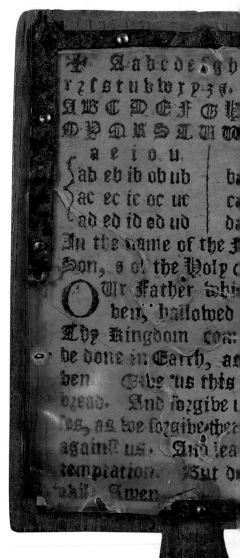

Above: *A horn book. The printed page is covered by a clear sheet made from an animal's horn, which protects it. The alphabet has no letter "j" ("i" was used instead, so the name John, for example, would be written Iohn), but it does have two extra symbols between the lower case "r" and "s" which are not in the modern alphabet. They are different ways of writing "s". The ordinary "s" is only used if it is the last letter of a word. If it comes anywhere else, one of the first two symbols are used.*

Above: *A Tudor school. Beating children is thought to be the best way of making them learn, and pupils who make mistakes in their lessons are usually punished in this way.*

Lessons

Latin and Divinity (religious education) are the most important subjects. A boy who wants a career in the church, law or medicine must be able to speak and write Latin. William and Robert read books by Latin authors like Virgil and Cicero, and write essays and poems in Latin. In Divinity lessons, they learn passages from the Bible by heart. William and Robert also learn Greek, arithmetic and music. They write with quill pens on parchment, and need to sharpen their quills every day with special "penknives".

Below: *Tudor handwriting. This letter was written by Princess Elizabeth to Queen Mary.*

beseche your higthnes to pardon · this my boldnes wiche mnocecy procures me to do toogther with hope of your nathyal kindnis wiche I trust wyl not se me cast away without deserf wiche what it is I woln desier no more of God but that yo

29

EATING AND DRINKING

L iving on a farm, Alice and Katherine make butter and cheese instead of buying it from the shops like townspeople. But wherever they live, Elizabethans can only eat what is "in season" at that particular time of year because they are not able to refrigerate their food to keep it fresh. When Harry kills animals in the autumn, Alice salts the meat and packs it in barrels for the family to eat during the winter. This meat often goes bad, so Alice makes spicey sauces to disguise its horrible taste.

Alice is a good cook. She makes dishes of roast and boiled veal, beef and chicken for her family and coloppes (slices of bacon) for the husbandmen. She also makes meat pies and stews, cheese tarts and fish dishes. Although the Baillys have lots of vegetables in their pottages and sallets (*see page 18*), vegetables were not popular with the nobility until the end of the sixteenth century, and people at court had an unhealthy diet with too much meat and salt.

Alice sometimes makes a fruit pie for pudding. She uses honey as a sweetener. Sugar, which is bought in large cone-shaped lumps, is becoming more popular although it is expensive. At court, where large amounts of sugar are added to the ale and used in meat and fish dishes and in sweetmeats such as marchpane (marzipan), people's teeth are beginning to rot and turn black (*see page 42*).

Fish Days

On Fridays and Saturdays, and at Lent (the 40 days before Easter) and Advent (the four weeks before Christmas), the Baillys eat fish instead of meat. This is because these days are "fast days" or "fish days" when there is a law forbidding people to eat meat. This law was made when England was a Catholic country. When Elizabeth I, a Protestant (*see page 5*), came to the throne, it was kept in the law books because it helped the fishermen's business, but it was not strictly enforced. However, the Baillys still obey it because eating fish helps them to preserve their stocks of meat. People who live near the coast eat sea-fish, but as these cannot be transported very far before they go rotten, those who live inland eat fish from rivers and special fishponds.

Above and left: *This "ark" is used to store bread. It is constructed so that neither mice nor damp can get into it. Alice bakes two kinds of bread in her bake-oven: "manchet"(white bread) and "cheat" (light brown bread).*

Left: *The pantry, where Alice churns butter and makes cheese. Food and cooking equipment is stored here, and ale is stored in a barrel.*

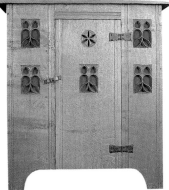

Above: *Alice and Katherine pick onions, string them together and hang them up. They cut one off when they need it.*

Left: *Alice keeps plates and cups in this cupboard.*

Below: *This herb and flower salad is made mainly of dandelion and daisy flowers and leaves. It also contains primrose flowers, sorrel, chopped fennel and leek, watercress, mint and rosemary. The pottage is made of peas, milk, egg yolks, breadcrumbs and parsley. It is flavoured with saffron and ginger.*

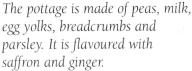

"To dinner we have a mess of pottage, new milk and fresh cheese, and to supper we have mutton sodde [boiled] with chopped herbs." Alice

Drinks

All the Baillys and their workers drink ale, brewed by Alice, with breakfast, dinner and supper. "Ale" is the Tudor name for any fermented drink made from malted grain and water. Beer, which was brewed with hops, is also drunk, but not as much as ale. The Baillys also drink cider (made from apples), perry (made from pears), mead (made from honey and spices) and posset, which is a mixture of eggs, milk and ale. They do not drink wine, which is drunk only by noblemen. Everybody avoids drinking water because it is polluted and makes them ill.

DINNER

Dinner is the most important meal in the Bailly household, and it is eaten at 12 noon. The evening meal, supper, is at 7pm in the winter, but later in the summer because Harry, Thomas, John and Richard work in the fields until dusk. The gentry, who do not have to fit their eating hours around their work, eat dinner at 11am and supper at 5pm. Supper is a smaller, lighter meal than dinner.

Right: *The Baillys' table is set for dinner.*

Below: *A pickled herring and fruit pie with pea pottage, jumbles (knotted biscuits) and posset to drink.*

Right: *These flat wooden objects are called "trenchers" and John and Richard use them as plates. Their meat is put in the big hollow in the centre. Some trenchers have a small hollow at one side to fill up with salt.*

Tableware

Poor people have wooden plates but richer families like the Baillys have pewter ones *(shown below)*. The biggest plates are called platters. The smaller ones are saucers, and they are used to hold sauces and dressings. The small dishes with two handles like ears are called porringers and they are used for pottage. The Baillys drink out of earthenware cups.

The Baillys all carry their own knives, and use them to cut up their food before picking it up in their fingers to eat. For eating pottage, they use spoons. Forks are very unusual. Some rich families have a set of fancy forks for eating sticky sweetmeats, but there are none in the Bailly household.

Table Manners

A book was published in 1557 which gave these rules for good table manners, but the Baillys, like most Elizabethans, are not very concerned about following them:

"Thy mouth not to full when thou dost eate;
Not smackynge thy lyppes, as commonly do hogges,
Nor gnawynge the bones as it were dogges; ...
Pyke not thy teethe at the table syttynge,
Nor use at thy meate over muche spytynge..."

(Do not overfill your mouth when you eat, Do not smack your lips like a pig, or gnaw bones like a dog... Do not pick your teeth when sitting at the table, or spit too much while you are eating...)

Jumbles

This recipe comes from a cookery book called *The Good Huswife's Jewell*, written by Thomas Dawson in 1596. He spells jumbles as "iombils".

1½oz (40g) salted butter
1 tablespoon rose water
4 oz (115g) caster sugar
1 tablespoon caraway seed
2 eggs
8oz (230g) plain flour

Beat the butter and rose water, add the sugar, and cream them together. Beat the eggs and add them, then add the spices and flour to make a soft dough. Knead the dough on a floured board and make it into about 15 simple knots, twists or rings. Put them on a buttered baking sheet. Bake in the oven (180°C, 350°F, gas mark 4) for 15-20 minutes. When they are golden, remove them from the oven and put them on a wire rack to cool.

GOING TO MARKET

Once a week, Alice walks to the local town to sell butter, cheese and eggs at the market. The market hall (*see right*) is crowded with traders, farmers' wives and townspeople doing their shopping. People are pushing and jostling, pigs are wandering about getting in everyone's way and the town crier is shouting out the latest news. If she hears anything interesting, Alice will tell Harry when she gets home.

Many country people do not go to market, but to one of the big fairs which are held two or three times each year. As well as foodstuffs, livestock is sold at these fairs and there are jugglers, acrobats and pedlars offering trinkets, ribbons and ballad sheets for sale.

Right: Goods are sold in the open arcade at the bottom of this market hall, and the town council meet in the room on the first floor.

Above: *Elizabethan market hall.*

Coinage

The picture below shows Elizabethan pound coins. There are also shillings, worth 12 pence each. There are 20 shillings to £1. "Groats" are worth four pence, and there are pennies, half-pennies and farthings, worth a quarter of a penny. "Marks" are worth 160 pence, and "half-marks" 80 pence.

CRIME AND PUNISHMENT

While she is at the market, Alice sees a beggar being whipped through the streets. This is a common sight, as there are many homeless people. By law, they are meant to stay in their home towns. Those who are caught wandering about the country begging are whipped and sometimes put in the stocks before being sent back to their own parish. There is no police force, but each county has a sheriff who has the job of arresting people accused of crimes and holding them in jail until their trial. If they escape, he has to pay a fine. They are then tried by the Justices of the Peace (JPs) in the local court. There are constables and officers of the watch who patrol the streets breaking up fights and investigating disturbances, but if a wanted criminal is on the loose in the neighbourhood the JPs declare a "hue and cry" and Harry and the other men are expected to come and help catch him. Whipping and fines are common punishments, but heretics and people found guilty of treason are usually burnt alive (*see page 36*), and murderers are often sentenced to be hanged, drawn and quartered. Noblemen and women are allowed to be beheaded – if the executioner is good at his job, this is a much quicker, less painful death.

Above: *Criminals are locked up in the small room below the market hall stairs.*

Above: *Women who are found guilty of witchcraft are often hanged or drowned. People are afraid that witches will put spells on them and make their crops fail and their animals and children die.*

RELIGION

Harry Bailly was born in 1540, and during his life the religion of England has changed from Catholic to Protestant, back to Catholic and then back again to Protestant. Each king or queen insisted that their religion was the only true one, and people must follow it. These changes do not worry Harry. Like most Tudors, he accepts that he must obey the king or queen, because that is God's law. He thinks that the king or queen has the right to tell him what to believe and how to worship – if he does what he is told, God will not punish him.

Religion plays a big part in the lives of Tudor people like the Baillys. When they were babies, their parents had to have them baptised, and as children they learnt prayers, the catechism (*see page 28*) and the Ten Commandments. By law, they must attend their parish church every Sunday, and they must marry in that church and be buried in its churchyard when they die. The churchwardens make sure that the people in the parish behave themselves, go to church and do not "break the Sabbath" by working.

Above: *People who refuse to change their religion are called heretics. When heretics are put on trial, they are given a chance to "recant" (say that they are mistaken in their beliefs). If they do not, they are usually burnt at the stake. Queen Mary, who was a staunch Catholic, burned many Protestants who refused to change their religion. This picture shows Thomas Cranmer, a leading Protestant, being burnt.*

When Henry VIII became head of the English Church, he became the owner of all the church property. Henry thought that the monks and nuns had become lazy and no longer cared about religion, and he needed money, so he closed down the religious houses and sold off their lands. Fountains Abbey in Yorkshire (*shown above*) was destroyed during the "dissolution" of the monasteries.

HEALTH AND MEDICINE

L ike most Tudor people, the Baillys rarely wash themselves or their clothes. Their house has a lavatory (*see page 43*) but most people go to the toilet wherever they happen to be – in streets (*see below*), fields, or in chamber pots and fireplaces when they are indoors. In the towns, people empty their rubbish straight into the street, and there are piles of animal dung everywhere. Outside butchers' shops, there are rotting animal carcasses which attract swarms of flies. Nobody understands about germs, which spread very easily, causing disease. The worst diseases are the plague, the "sweating sickness" and smallpox (*see page 46*). Only the rich can afford to have physicians – who, in any case, are as likely to kill their patients as cure them – and the Baillys, like most people, use herbal remedies. Some herbs are thought to be particularly good for you. Garlic, for example, is called "the poor man's physic" (medicine).

Above: Alice uses sweet-smelling herbs to try and hide the smell of unwashed people and sewage.

Left: A medicine jar

Above: The Bible in English. Before Tudor times, Bibles were in Latin, and few people could read them. Protestants thought that everyone should be able to read the Bible for themselves, but Catholics disagreed because they thought it would make people start to think about what the Bible said and question it. At the start of Henry VIII's reign, anyone caught with an English Bible was burnt at the stake. Protestant King Edward VI allowed the English Bible to be read, but Queen Mary forbade it. It is encouraged under Elizabeth I.

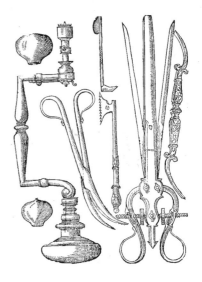

Above right: Surgical instruments. "Barber surgeons", who are hairdressers as well as surgeons, amputate limbs and set broken bones. There are no anaesthetics or pain-killers, so people who need to have an operation are given a lot of alcohol to drink and held down by the surgeon's helpers while he cuts them open. Many illnesses are thought to be caused by bad blood, and "blood letting", which means cutting open a vein and letting the blood out, is a popular cure. People also think that it helps them to get rid of their sins.

GAMES AND SPORTS

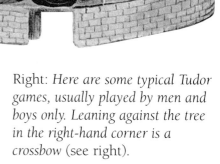

Left: *A cockpit.*

Like their clothes (*see page 16*), the games people can play are regulated. John, Richard and the other husbandmen are not allowed to play skittles, tennis, bowls or any similar game unless they have permission from a JP (*see page 35*) or unless it is Christmas, when they can play if Harry Bailly is present. As they work for long hours they have little time for sport, except for their archery practice (*see opposite page*). Sometimes they join in a game of football. A blown-up pig's bladder serves as a ball, and the goal posts can be as much as three miles apart – sometimes in different villages. The ball can be kicked, thrown or carried. There is no limit to the number of players, and they can tackle by punching, tripping or simply grabbing hold of the person with the ball. People are often injured playing football, and sometimes even killed. Gentlemen and noblemen do not play football because they think that it is a low sport, but it is very popular with the villagers.

Like many farmers, Harry keeps a fighting cock in his yard, and enjoys going to cockfights. These are very popular, as is the sport of bear-baiting, where people watch a tethered bear fighting off attacks from dogs.

Right: *Here are some typical Tudor games, usually played by men and boys only. Leaning against the tree in the right-hand corner is a crossbow (see right).*

Above: *Tennis, like bowls, was a sport for gentlemen. It was played indoors, with leather balls stuffed with hair. Rich people had bowling alleys and tennis courts attached to their houses.*

Archery

Parliament encourages men like John and Richard to practise archery, which they are supposed to do on Sundays and holy days (*see page 40*). This is because good archers are important in wartime, and the government is concerned that too much practice time is spent on other sports and that the bow makers and fletchers (arrow makers) may go out of business as a result. They are also worried that crossbows are becoming more popular than the traditional longbows, so a law has been passed saying that only wealthy landowners can use them.

Above: *The fletchings (feathers) of an arrow.*

Below: *Equipment for making arrows.*

"It is a pleasant sport to see the bear defend himself from the dogs with all his force and skill, throwing down all who come within his reach."
Harry

Left: *Stag hunts are popular with the nobility, as are jousting tournaments like the one shown here. Knights on horseback rush at each other on either side of a barrier, trying to knock one another off their horses with lances, while the ladies of the court cheer on their favourites.*

ENTERTAINMENTS

T he Baillys do not have much leisure time because they work hard and do not stay up very late at night. Katherine is a good singer, and she sometimes entertains the family after supper. Thomas buys her songsheets with new ballads to sing.

Thomas enjoys the new habit of smoking tobacco in a long clay pipe, which is becoming very popular. Some physicians say that smoking is good for you, but others argue that it is bad for your health. Harry doesn't smoke because he says "it is good for nothing but to choke a man and fill him full of smoke and soot".

Right: *The Baillys drink their ale from beakers made of animal horn and big leather jugs.*

Above right: *Gambling on cards and dice is popular, especially amongst the nobility. Backgammon, which is known as "tables", and dominoes are enjoyed by many people.*

Holy Days and Feast Days

Every month there are several holy days, when people are not allowed to work, but must attend church. When they get home, they usually have a feast. Although the year officially begins on March 25th, January 1st, which is a holy day, is still known as New Year's Day. The Baillys look forward particularly to Shrove Tuesday, when they can toss pancakes and join in the big football match in the village. They also enjoy Easter, Whitsun, the Harvest Festival, All Hallows Eve (Hallowe'en) and Christmas. As well as holy days, there are also festivals which have nothing to do with the church, such as May Day, when people dance around a maypole, and Midsummer's Eve.

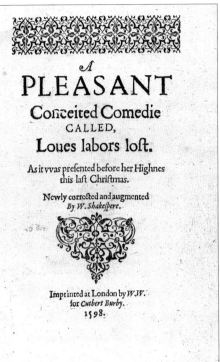

A
PLEASANT
Conceited Comedie
CALLED,
Loues labors loft.

As it vvas prefented before her Highnes
this laft Chriftmas.

Newly corrected and augmented
By W. Shakespere.

Imprinted at London by W.W.
for Cutbert Burby.
1598.

Above: *The title page of* Love's
Labour's Lost, *one of
Shakespeare's early comedies.
Amongst his most famous plays
are* Hamlet, Macbeth, The
Merchant of Venice *and* A
Midsummer Night's Dream.

Left: *People at all levels of
society enjoy dancing. The Baillys
and their neighbours dance
country dances. Elizabeth I
loves dancing, and the
volta (shown here) is one
of the popular dances at
her court. People dance
to music played on lutes
(similar to guitars),
virginals (similar to
pianos), flutes, recorders,
drums and viols (stringed
instruments like violins).*

Plays

In the 1560s, when Harry was a young man, he saw plays acted by companies of travelling actors who performed in market squares and the courtyards of inns. These actors wandered from town to town and would be arrested and treated in the same way as beggars (*see page 35*) if they were caught. However, since that time, several theatres have been built in the larger towns, especially London, and the profession of player (actor) has become more respectable. All players are men, as women are not allowed to go on the stage. The theatre attracts both rich and poor, and there are many exciting plays to see by writers such as William Shakespeare (*see left*). Most Elizabethan plays are extremely violent, with scenes of killing and torture. This is partly because they are in competition with bear-baitings (*see page 38*). The audience can buy apples, pears and nuts to eat while they watch.

BEDTIME

Harry and Thomas close the shutters. It is pitch dark outside, and fairly dark inside the house as well because the Baillys' rushlights and candles do not give out much light. Harry and Alice sleep in the "best" bed *(shown opposite and below right)*. It is a four-poster bed with a cloth tester (ceiling) and curtains which help to keep out draughts. The small bed underneath it is called a truckle bed. It stays under the best bed during the day and is wheeled out at night for William and Robert. It is very common for Tudor children to share a bedroom with their parents. Thomas and Katherine sleep in the "second best" bed *(shown far right)*. Edward's cradle is next to it. Richard and John sleep on mattresses called "pallets" which are stuffed with straw.

Above left: *Strong cords hold the mattresses in place.*

Above right: *There are two mattresses: a thin bottom one made from plaited straw and a softer, thicker top one (shown folded back). This is filled with flock (wool which is not good enough to spin), as are the pillows. The straw mattress is strewn with herbs to make the bed smell nice. The blankets are made of wool and decorated with a blue band at each end, and the sheets are made of linen.*

Washing

If the Baillys want to wash, which is not very often, they have to fetch water from the well *(see page 11)*. Alice makes soap from a mixture of ash, quicklime and animal fat.

Like many Elizabethans, the Baillys do not clean their teeth, and their breath smells horrible. Thomas has toothache, so he is going to ask the the barber surgeon *(see page 37)* to pull out the rotten tooth with a pair of tongs. Some people clean their teeth with a mixture of honey, vinegar and wine which they rub on with their fingers. Those who are rich enough can buy tooth scrapers that look like tiny sickles. Some people ask the barber surgeon to put "aqua fortis" (nitric acid) on their teeth to whiten them. This is a bad idea because nitric acid is corrosive and destroys their teeth by eating through them.

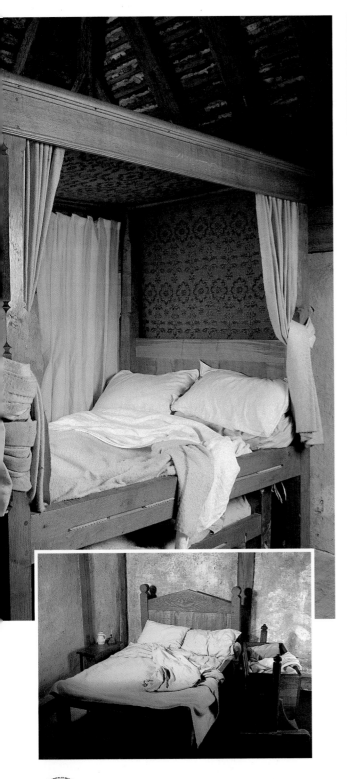

Above: *The inside of the Baillys' garderobe.*

Right: *The outside of the garderobe. The waste pit has a bed of ashes at the bottom. When it is full, the contents of the pit are emptied out, mixed with the ashes and spread on the garden as fertilizer.*

Garderobes

A Tudor toilet is known as a garderobe, a privy or a jakes. The Baillys' garderobe *(shown above)* is a plank with a hole in it, fixed on to the outside of their house. It does not have a waste pipe, but empties straight into the pit outside. There is no toilet paper, so the Baillys sometimes use large leaves instead *(shown right)*. There is a special pot for urine *(shown above right)*, which is saved because it is useful for bleaching fabric and fixing dye (making it permanent).

"We have been long at supper. Let us say evening prayers and go to bed in God's name."
Harry

43

THE HOUSE IN TIME

The Baillys' house and farm were built in 1565 and the family lived there for the rest of the Tudor era. Here are some of the events that took place in Britain before, during and after this date, in the reign of the Tudor monarchs Henry VII, Henry VIII, Edward VI, Mary I and Elizabeth I.

1485 The Battle of Bosworth Field ends the Wars of the Roses. Henry Tudor defeats Richard III and is crowned Henry VII, the first Tudor king.
Sweating sickness breaks out in England.

1492 Christopher Columbus lands in America.

1501 Henry VII marries his eldest son Arthur to Catherine of Aragon, a Spanish Princess.

1502 Death of Arthur.

1504 The first pocket watch is made in Germany.

1508 British explorer Sebastian Cabot sails into Hudson Bay, North America.

1509 Death of Henry VII. Henry VIII becomes king aged 18. He marries Catherine of Aragon.

1512 James IV of Scotland invades England.

1513 Scotland defeated. James IV killed. His young son James V becomes king.

1516 Catherine of Aragon gives birth to Mary I.

1517 Second outbreak of the sweating sickness in England. In some towns, half the people die from it.

1525 William Tyndale translates the New Testament into English. It is illegally smuggled into England from the Netherlands.

1528 Third outbreak of the sweating sickness in England. Two thousand people die in London alone.

1533 Henry VIII divorces Catherine of Aragon and marries Anne Boleyn. He is excommunicated (expelled) from the Catholic Church by the Pope.
Anne Bolyen gives birth to Elizabeth I.

1534 The Act of Supremacy is passed, making Henry the head of the English Church.

1536 Anne Boleyn is beheaded. Henry VIII marries Jane Seymour.
The people rebel against the enclosure of common land.

1536-1539 Dissolution of the monasteries.

1537 Jane Seymour dies after giving birth to Edward VI.

1540 Henry VIII marries, and then divorces, Anne of Cleves. He then marries Catherine Howard.
Birth of Harry Bailly.

1541 Henry VIII has Catherine Howard beheaded.

1542 Scotland and England at war. The Scots are defeated at Solway Moss. Death of James V. His daughter Mary becomes queen. She is one week old.

1543 Henry VIII marries Catherine Parr, who outlives him.

1546 English troops are sent to Scotland to try and force a marriage between Mary, Queen of Scots, and Henry VIII's son Edward. They are unsuccessful.

1547 Death of Henry VIII. Edward VI becomes king. Edward Seymour, Duke of Somerset becomes Lord Protector.

1549 The Act of Uniformity is passed and the first English prayer book is introduced.

1550 The Duke of Somerset is imprisoned and the Duke of Northumberland becomes the new Lord Protector.
Law passed introducing "abiding places" (workhouses) in each parish for the relief of the poor.

1551 Fourth outbreak of the sweating sickness.

1552 Act passed authorizing "Collectors of Charitable Alms" to call on people each week and collect money they had promised to give for the relief of the destitute poor.

1553 Edward VI dies aged 15 having named the Protestant Lady Jane Grey as his successor. After nine days as queen she is overthrown by Mary and imprisoned. Mary I becomes queen and reinstates the Catholic Church. She has over 300 Protestants burnt as heretics.

1554 Mary I marries Phillip II of Spain. Lady Jane Grey is beheaded.
Birth of Alice Bailly.

1558 Mary I dies. Elizabeth I becomes queen, aged 25.

1559 New Act of Supremacy makes Elizabeth I head of the English Church. England becomes a Protestant country again.

1560 Mary, Queen of Scots lays claim to the English throne. She becomes a focus for Catholic rebellion against Elizabeth I. Jean Nicot introduces tobacco into Europe from America.

1563 Act of 39 Articles passed setting out Church of England doctrine. A severe outbreak of plague causes 17,046 deaths . in London.

1564 Birth of William Shakespeare.

1565 First pencil made in Switzerland.

1567 Mary, Queen of Scots flees to England after a Protestant rebellion in Scotland. She is imprisoned.
The Baillys' house is built.

1568 Birth of Thomas Bailly.
Flemish map-maker Mercator introduces the modern method of drawing maps.

1570 Birth of Katherine Bailly.

1570 Elizabeth I excommunicated. English Catholics come under suspicion when the Pope tells them that it is their duty to depose her.
Persistent attacks by English sailors on Spanish ships lead to worsening relations between the two countries.

1576 The first theatre in London is built.

1577 Francis Drake begins his journey around the world. He returns in 1580.

1578 Birth of physician William Harvey, who discovered that the heart pumps blood around the body.

1579 Harry and Alice Bailly are married.

1580 Birth of William Bailly.
Around this date, the potato is introduced into Europe from South America by the Spaniards.

1583 Birth of Robert Bailly.

1587 Mary, Queen of Scots executed for treason.

1588 The defeat of the Armada.

1589 Thomas and Katherine Bailly are married.

1590 Birth of Edward Bailly.

1592 The first Shakespeare play performed. By 1603, 24 of Shakespeare's plays had been performed in London, including *Romeo and Juliet* and *Hamlet*. Italian scientist Galileo Galilei builds a telescope which magnifies objects 30 times.

1595 Sir Walter Raleigh sails to Guiana, South America, looking for the legendary city made of gold, El Dorado. He does not find it.

1596 Sir John Harrington invents the flushing toilet, but nobody takes it seriously. The idea does not catch on for over 200 years.

1597 An act is passed making it illegal not to give money for the relief of the poor. Those who refuse to pay the Collectors are imprisoned.

1600 The foundation of the East India Company leads to an increase in trade overseas.

1603 Elizabeth I dies, aged 70. James VI of Scotland, son of Mary, Queen of Scots, becomes James I of England. He is the first of the Stuart monarchs.
Serious outbreak of the plague – over 38,000 people die in London.

GLOSSARY

Baptism The ceremony performed when someone, usually a baby, becomes a member of the Christian religion. The person is either sprinkled with, or immersed in, water as a symbol of the washing away of their sins.

Catholic Member of a Christian religion that is headed by the Pope in Rome, Italy. Catholics believe that the Pope represents God on earth. Catholic churches are highly decorated with statues and pictures.

Corset A stiffened, tight-fitting undergarment which is designed to give the wearer, usually a woman, a slim waist.

Dissolution Ending or destroying by breaking up or 'dissolving'. Under Henry VIII laws were passed ordering the dissolution of the monasteries (*see page 36*). The monks and nuns were sent away and their money and church ornaments were seized by the king's officers. Religious statues were destroyed, stained glass windows broken and some parts of the buildings themselves were knocked down and removed.

Enclosure Country people who did not own land kept their few cows, pigs and hens on common land (*see page 7*). During the Tudor era, landowners found that they could make more money farming sheep for their wool than from growing crops, so they began to enclose (fence off) common land so they could graze their sheep on it. The poor people were furious because this meant that they had nowhere to keep their animals. Many of them lost their jobs as farm labourers, and could not get other work because sheep do not need many people to look after them.

Excommunication A sentence passed on someone by the Pope, expelling them from the Catholic Church.

When someone is excommunicated, they are not allowed to attend Church or have prayers said for them by the Church. Catholics believe that people who are excommunicated will not be able to go to Heaven when they die.

Fallow Land which is not sown with seed is said to "lie fallow" (*see pages 19 and 25*). Land is left unseeded so that it can rest and regain its fertility in order that the next seeds sown on it will produce a good crop

Harrow A farming tool which is used to make the ground level, break up clods of earth and destroy weeds before crops are planted (*see page 24*).

Heir A person who will inherit somebody's title, money and property when they die.

Heretic Someone whose religious beliefs differ from the established teachings of his or her Church (*see page 36*).

Hops The dried, ripe flowers of the hop plant which are used in the making of beer.

Parish A small area, such as a village, which has its own church, clergyman and local government officials.

Pedlar A person who travels from place to place selling goods.

Plague A widespread, highly contagious and fatal disease which was spread by rat fleas. There was no cure for the plague, which killed huge numbers of people (*see page 45*). In an effort to stop the spread of infection, a law was passed that all houses where someone had died of plague must keep their doors and windows closed for 40 days. These houses had to be marked with a cross and the words "Lord, have mercy upon us" so that people would know not to come near them. In some towns, plague victims were carried outside the walls and left to die in the fields so that they could not infect any more people.

Platter A large plate which is used for serving food.

Pottage A thick soup, usually made with vegetables (*see page 30*).

Protestant Originally, someone who protested against the teachings and organization of the Catholic Church. Protestants in England recognize the monarch, not the Pope, as head of the Church. They prefer simple churches, without statues or pictures. In Tudor times, they encouraged the use of the English Bible instead of the Latin one (*see page 37*).

Rafters Wooden beams that are the framework of a roof.

Ruff Large circular pleated collar, often starched, worn around the neck by Elizabethan men and women.

Sheriff Sheriffs, who were always men, were knights or gentlemen, and were chosen by the monarch. They were responsible for local government and keeping order.

Sickle A farming tool with a curved blade which is used for cutting grass or corn.

Smallpox A highly contagious illness which was often fatal in Tudor times. The symptoms are fever and spots on the skin. A survivor of smallpox was often left with pitted marks on his or her skin where the spots had been.

Stocks These were heavy wooden frames with holes into which wrongdoers' feet were put. The stocks were then locked so that they could not move. People were usually punished for minor crimes by being made to sit in the stocks for several days. While they were in the stocks, local people came by to jeer at them and pelted them with rotten food.

Sumptuary Controlling extravagant spending. The Tudor Sumptuary Laws stopped people spending money on luxurious clothes (*see page 17*).

Sundial A device for measuring time by a pointer which throws a shadow onto a flat surface which is marked with the hours. As sundials depend on having enough light to show a shadow, they can only work during the hours of daylight. Unlike a clock which shows the hours going round from one to 12, sundials generally start at five or six when the sun rises in the morning, and go round to six or seven, when it sets. Most sundials were quite large, but sailors sometimes had small ones which they carried around in their pockets.

Sweating Sickness People were suddenly affected by this strange disease which was also known as 'the Sweat'. It could kill within as little as 10 or 12 hours in very bad cases. Those who were still alive after 24 hours of profuse sweating and high fever usually survived. As with most diseases in Tudor times, there was no effective treatment for it.

Treason The crime of betraying one's monarch or country. A person who is guilty of treason is called a traitor.

The Wars of the Roses Before the Tudor period, there had been 30 years of fighting between two rival parts of the royal family over who should be king of England. These battles were known as the Wars of the Roses because one faction, the House of Lancaster, had a red rose as its emblem, and the other, the House of York, had a white rose. The Wars of the Roses ended when Lancastrian Henry Tudor defeated Yorkist King Richard III at the Battle of Bosworth in 1485. Richard III was killed in the battle, and Henry Tudor was crowned King Henry VII. He married the daughter of a Yorkist king, Edward IV, to make sure that nobody would be able to challenge his descendent's claim to the throne.

Wattle and Daub Woven twigs (wattle) covered with a mixture of clay, lime, cow-dung and chopped straw (daub), used for building walls.

INDEX

PLACES TO VISIT

BURGHLEY HOUSE
Stamford, Lincolnshire
01780 52451
Late Elizabethan manor house.

GREAT DIXTER
Northiam, East Sussex
01797 253160
15th century half-timbered manor house.

HAMPTON COURT PALACE
35 Hampton Street, London SE17 3AN
0181 781 9500
Built by Cardinal Wolsey and taken over by Henry VIII for use as a royal palace.

HARDWICK HALL
nr Chesterfield, Derbyshire
01246 850430
Built in the 1590s, with a collection of furniture, needlework and tapestries.

HATFIELD HOUSE
Hatfield, Hertfordshire
01707 262823
Tudor wing where Elizabeth I lived before she became queen.

HOLYROOD PALACE
Edinburgh, Scotland EH8 8DX
0131 556 7371
Home of Mary, Queen of Scots.

LITTLE MORETON HALL
Congleton, Cheshire CW12 4SD
01260 272018
Timber framed manor house, begun in the 15th century.

HEVER CASTLE
Edenbridge, Kent TN8 7NG
01732 865224
Childhood home of Anne Boleyn.

KENTWELL HALL
Long Melford, Suffolk
01787 310207
Red brick moated Tudor manor house with walled garden.

MARY ROSE EXHIBIT
H.M. Naval Base, College Road,
Portsmouth PO1 3LX
01705 750521
Displays relating to the contents of the Mary Rose, a ship sunk in the time of Henry VIII.

MUSEUM OF LONDON
150 London Wall, London EC2Y 5HN
0181 332 1141
Displays relating to London in Tudor times.

OXBURGH HALL
Oxburgh, Norfolk PE33 9PS
0136 621258
Late 15th century moated house.

PAYCOCKE'S
West Street, Essex CO6 1NS
01376 561305
Merchant's house, dating from 1500.

SHAKESPEARE'S GLOBE MUSEUM
New Globe Walk, Bankside, London SE1
0171 928 6406
Exhibition on the rebuilding of the Elizabethan Globe Theatre.

SUTTON HOUSE
2-4 Homerton High Street, London E9 6JQ
0181 986 2264
16th century town house.

TUDOR MERCHANT'S HOUSE
Tenby, Dyfed, Wales CF8 1JL
01834 842279
15th century merchant's house.

WEALD AND DOWNLAND OPEN AIR MUSEUM
Singleton, Chichester, West Sussex
01243 811348
Collection of historic buildings from the Weald and Downland area, including a Tudor house and market hall.

Acknowledgements

Breslich & Foss would like to thank **Michelle Green, Christopher Zeuner** and the staff of the **Weald and Downland Open Air Musem**.

Picture Credits

All photographs were taken at the **Weald and Downland Open Air Museum** except those listed below.
Bodleian Library, University of Oxford p.28-29 (centre)
Bridgeman Art Library p.4-5 (top centre) Private Collection / Bridgeman Art Library, p.16-17 (top centre) Burghley House, Stamford, Lincolnshire / Bridgeman Art Library pp.40-41 (top centre) Collection of the Earl of Derby, Suffolk / Bridgeman Art Library
British Library p.7 (centre), p.16 (top right), p.17 (centre), p.36 (top left), p.41 (top right)
The College of Arms pp.38-39 (bottom)
Edinburgh University Library p. 38 (top)
The Folger Shakespeare Library p.39 (top centre)
Fotomas Index p. 6 (centre left) and p.37 (centre)
Hulton Deutsch Collection p. 29 (top right)
Jarrold Publishing p.28 (top left)
Mansell Collection p.6 (bottom right), p.7 (bottom centre), p.35 (bottom right)
Mary Rose Trust p.16 (bottom centre)
Museum of London p.37 bottom centre
The National Portrait Gallery p.4 (left and bottom right), p.5 (centre and top right)
The National Gallery p.16 (top left)
The National Trust Photographic Library p.36 bottom right
The Royal Collection © Her Majesty the Queen pp.36-37 (top centre)
Royal Mint p.34 bottom left
Collection of the Marquis of Salisbury, Hatfield House, Herts © Marquis of Salisbury p.6-7 (centre)
Tate Gallery, London p.26-27 (top centre)
The Wellcome Trust p.37 (centre right)

Riddle on page 27: The answer is "A man sits on a stool with a leg of mutton in his lap. A dog snatches the leg of mutton and runs away with it. The man picks up the stool and throws it at the dog, who brings back the leg of mutton."

The quotations in this book are adapted from *The Elizabethan Home* discovered in two dialogues by Claudius Hollyband and Peter Erondell, ed. M. St. Clare Byrne, London 1925 and *Tudor Family Portrait*, B. Winchester, London 1955.

Please note that eating dandelions, daisies and other wild flowers could be harmful and is not recommended.